The Default Setting

Is Love

A story told in many pieces

Poems of common threads
running through us all

Showing why the revolution of modern life
is intelligent, moral and beautiful

Thomas Dexter Kerr

2018 Edition

First Published
September 2014

ISBN-13: 978-1505229073

Also by Thomas Dexter Kerr:

The Origin of Intelligence:
 The Role of Information in Everyday Life

Published by Nova Science Publishers   2009

thomasdexterkerr.com

For Donna

Preface

Why the revolution of modern life
is intelligent, moral and beautiful

It is an exciting and hopeful time to be alive. A revolution is sweeping the earth, increasing intelligence by allowing, enabling, inspiring ever more people to make more decisions in their lives. Modern systems that allow people to think more in daily life are well known. Democracies empower people to choose governments. Markets are people deciding what should be made and done. Systems of rules that apply to all help keep things open and honest. Support for ability to think comes from family and neighbors, schools, hospitals, books and internet. Enormous dividends result from getting it right. But decentralizing decision-making is never easy because it means ever greater complexity and the empowering of inconvenient people. The best path forward is illuminated by the idea that people thinking more is good, right and beautiful.

Modern peace and prosperity has resulted from the ever closer alignment of social organization with ways people by nature maximize intelligence. Humans became the most powerful beings ever to exist by developing a new way of using information, the content of thoughts and feelings. The information system created as people mingle thoughts and feelings with those of others evolved to be the most intelligent entity ever to exist.

Survival of the fittest individual was not the primary force that crafted human minds. Incompetence in a wide variety of forms is an essential part of what makes us human. Individual people today lack the full range of mental abilities necessary to survive alone in a wilderness. I couldn't do it, nor could any of my neighbors. Instead natural selection resulted in something far more powerful, intelligent and beautiful.

Many creatures, from ants to dogs, evolved to gain power over their environment by cooperating and communicating. All lost the ability to live and thrive alone as individuals. Over eons, humans gradually took the use of information to higher levels. As individuals they gave up the full range of faculties needed for survival because together they developed something far more potent. The unprecedented power this gave them at each step is what drove the evolutionary innovations that resulted in today's world.

Human intelligence is collective in nature, talents not concentrated but dispersed in individuals who are all different. A revolutionary kind of mind developed in groups of a few hundred in which everyone knew each other, every voice added to what was being thought about. In everyday life people have always shared ideas, songs, stories, styles and a myriad nuances of feeling, passing them down through generations, improving and innovating. The information that is the content of thoughts and feelings mixes together in their minds and among them. Because each person's mind is different, enormous creative flexibility arises out of many sorts of thinking striving, sometimes clashing, always mingling. We spin thoughts out of the unknown and unexpected, finding depth and diversity with inauspicious people and rising generations breaking old patterns. So many things can be thought about. Human survival and success has always depended on the system of thoughts that all share and take part in. Our kind of intelligence is a category leap, rising far beyond what could ever evolve to be the smartest, most wily, most dominant individual beast. Every successful creature is over-endowed with the means it uses to survive, necessary to overcome extreme circumstances. Our primary means of survival blossomed into the wonder of the universe.

The details of how individuals think were shaped by

the enormous force of their effect on our primary tool and weapon, the human information system. Its intelligence could increase only as its component parts became more finely tuned to add to the thinking going on. Many of the talents that make people together so intelligent are useless in isolation, essential when combined with others. Kinds of thinking are scattered, each getting a little of this, a little of that. Impractical musicians, nonathletic priests, groveling politicians help bring disparate folks together. Mechanics fix things, clumsy scientists invent, cooks devise food, athletes run and hunt, shoppers gather, some who can memorize, memorialize the past. Fearless and timid, quick and slow, passive and aggressive, skillful and clumsy, female and male, serious and frivolous, analytical and intuitive, speculative and methodical, mathematical or musical or not, all are found in every group across the globe. This deep reservoir of possibilities is made more potent by the creativity inherent in the fresh perspectives of each individual and new generation. The mix found everywhere today exists because it is the combination that proved to be most intelligent.

If individuality were not naturally configured to mesh with other minds, the results would be useless. An association of thinking animals with a purely random assortment of differences would produce the intelligence of a zoo. Mental individuality in humans has a purpose. All elements are finely tuned to create with others, each general type essential, every new addition a welcome extension of the ability of everyone to think. It is an inescapable truth of every person's life that their most intimate impulses, those feelings that are most certainly theirs and theirs alone, are shaped and channeled in subtle, mysterious ways to augment the functioning of the human information system as a whole.

The magic of the human information system lies in everyday life, the great generator and heartland of intelligence. When a good idea pops into existence there is no way

9

to ever figure out exactly where it came from. Inside everyone the information that is the content of their thoughts and feelings connects and mingles. Music and sports mix with math, politics and sex. Interconnections multiply as thoughts and fragments spread out through friends and neighbors, reaching around the world. All ideas are composed of strands reaching far back in the past and over many lands, influenced by threads of rhythm, color and rhyme, outrageous mistakes and hallucinations. Even the loftiest, most abstract sophisticated concepts grow out of pieces rattling around coffee shops, nurseries and football fields, mixing with music, cooking and gardening. Every mind takes part, each one living in the thinking of the world. Together we create the mental output on which all depend.

Morality evolved as an inseparable part of intelligence. In order to think together, people have to get along. This is not automatic. Our existence through the past has always been dependent on a balance of genetic and cultural supports for moral behavior that maximizes the creative intelligence of the human information system. We are genetically predisposed to empathize with others, fall in love and like things like music and sports that join people together. But we also need ongoing streams of new ideas in all areas of life, good and bad, to be dreamed up and tried out. Our collective creativity relies on a diversity of individuals in all walks of life making different choices, going their own way. A measure of wildness, especially by teenagers, is built in. The resulting instability requires a lot of work. We inherit culture as much as we do fingers. Moral concepts in multiple forms have been passed down and improved on from primordial times in the same way as technical ideas like the use of fire. Without morality, just as without fire, everyone dies. Embedded in every culture is a way of understanding the information realities of life, some picture of lives connected by invisible ties in a common endeavor and fate, the furtherance of which is everyone's responsibility. This is contained in direct explanations as well as music and art, sports, humor and a thousand tales about others and the past. The enormous success of the human endeavor owes a lot to the efforts of so many through the ages searching for ever better ways to convince people to live together wholeheartedly.

Though it can be hard to include those who are different, closing eyes to them shuts off communion with thought itself. To regard anyone at all as unworthy of recognition is to turn away from intelligence, which exists in pieces scattered everywhere. Every face is a unique shining facet of the most complex thinking entity ever to exist. The greatest impediments to human potential are institutional, philosophical and viscerally emotional objections to getting little voices raised and heard. It seems so easy to disregard the shy, odd, peculiar and strange, both rebellious and those that sound the same, voices small and lonely, the less talented and nonpolitical. But they are us and we are all there is.

The revolution of modern life is vastly expanding intelligence by turning on its head traditional notions that the source of wealth and power is the best and brightest. What is emerging instead is a world in which every mind is acknowledged as an important contributor. Particular individuals are useful for any one task at hand, and when they manage to do something special it is a wonderful gift to themself and everyone else. But no matter how impressive, every success is the result of a limited, particular vision applied to resources drawn from the vast sea of human thought. Mental or character perfection is an attribute of people as a whole. Individuals are expressly designed not to be that way. Every individual can be described as 'flawed' or 'not perfect'. This is a good, not bad thing. The largest are dependent, the smallest have something to add. The most striking thing an honest person sees in mirrors is the amazing ordinariness of uniqueness. So-called ordinary people exist only because we were over eons in the most severe circumstances in fact essential to the intelligence of the whole. The most important and potent attribute of human intelligence is not that some are all-encompassing geniuses but that none are.

In the practical world of everyday life, people thinking is people making decisions. On a large scale decentralizing decision-making so more are thinking is difficult. As individuals choose who to marry, where to live and what to do for others they create ever greater complexity because they are all different. But only when they go in their own directions is the intelligence of society enriched by their diversity. For them to be allowed do so, they need to be trusted to make reasonably good decisions. Most people have to believe in doing the right thing. Their activities will at times need to be nudged or constrained in more positive directions. Growing a beautiful garden takes a lot of work.

Individual initiative would look morally suspect if human minds evolved mainly to compete against each other. Then their inner being would be suffused with primordial impulses to do so at others expense. Even if not in fact stealing, their motivation would be tainted with it. From that perspective, morality would be an overlay designed to counteract human nature and attempts to achieve general fairness would struggle against the tide. Such concepts provide handy excuses to keep people from acting, to confine them in a static order that is supposedly more moral. But because human minds did not in fact evolve to oppose others, exactly the opposite is true. In the practical world, this distinction has a huge effect, changing the role of rules from constraining people's base nature to facilitating greater activity with helpful guidelines and admonitions. Taking initiative is people thinking. Intelligence is the source of morality.

A functioning system of separate and independent organizations has an inherent beauty and morality that is lacking in the only alternative. The appeal of centralized systems is the supposed comfort of enforced fairness. Their slogans through the ages can sound idealistic: a place for everyone and everyone in their place, and we think and you do and we'll take care of you. This has been most attractive to those already privileged or who suppose themselves superior. It is just so hard to imagine what good could come from having stupid people think. But imposed absolute fairness is a state of standing still, bereft of creativity and initiative, missing the point of life. Visions of everyone nicely quiet and in order are nightmares not dreams, horror not paradise. Their imposition has resulted in police states and mass murder for they directly contravene the most fundamental human reality, that our destiny is to think. The great counter-revolution of modern times was communism, which sought to infuse old ideas with more effective means of control. Substitute a unitary bureaucracy for kings, emperors or caliphs and the concept is the same. In recent times it has been shown that more open systems are far more accountable, productive, able to experiment and vastly improve life. The reason it works better is because it is more intelligent. More people are thinking.

Capitalism is the use of math for the purpose of decentralizing decision-making. Math is an impartial tool for opening activities to anyone who wants to take initiative. To measure whether they are doing something worthwhile it empowers the most dispersed, appropriate and severe critics, customers. Pricing includes the user in the decision-making process, enlisting their mind to help make systems more intelligent. When people pay the true costs of the things they use, it is then they, instead of someone else, who is deciding how much and when. They have most say when they can choose from the widest selection in the world. From single entrepreneurs to enormous organizations, the proper use of math makes possible the most active use of people's minds. When capitalism strays too far from its decentralizing purpose it becomes dysfunctional and inefficient. When working well it is beautiful because it is intelligent.

Essential to success in business is finding the right balance between making money and serving others. Actually doing something worthwhile is hard, failure a constant shadow. All kinds of people need to be made happy enough to voluntarily cooperate. Customers, workers, neighbors, a variety of government folks, competitors, suppliers, contractors, all must get along. Every day brings hard choices between scarce resources and quality of output. Everything takes longer and costs more, no one is paid as much as they think they should, and temptations abound to take shortcuts. Episodes of winning the lottery and successful cheating make fun stories, but that's not where the real money is. Real business success is never only about maximizing profits. As human beings, business people connect with their world in many ways, have multiple interests and goals. Their job is to make an enterprise work as a whole, otherwise all is lost. Success requires doing and caring about two things at the same time. Many people's desires need to be filled and it all has to add up. Serve to make money, make money to serve, chew gum and walk.

An open democratic political system is a necessary component of an intelligent society. There will always be those tempted to recentralize decision-making in order to grab advantages for themselves or a select group. Democracy empowers the majority who are less interested in gaining power and dominance over others. However, their ability to make decisions in their own lives is very important to them. This can lead to wild cultural expressions because it is central to self worth and identity. Secondary objects like guns and cars can represent the rightness of individuals thinking for themselves. And in believing it is both moral and productive for them to live actively thinking, they are right. The greatest beneficiaries of a decentralized society are its less important members. Democracy puts the right hands on the tiller, those

14

most directly and personally interested in greater intelligence.

It is easy for initiatives to get out of hand, go in destructive directions. For capitalism to function it must have rules and guidance provided by an active democracy. All entrepreneurs, small to large, require ongoing adjustments to rules protecting their projects from theft and interference. They need an environment with sufficient infrastructure and healthy, educated citizens. They need the peaceful ways of solving problems that can thrive only in a functioning democratic political system with the good will of most of the people most of the time. Democratic capitalism is millions of people voluntarily cooperating and taking initiative to make life better for each other.

Democracy is commonly slandered as the worst system of governing except for every other. It involves a great show of shouting and grandstanding, confusion, indecision, delay, some cheating and lots of inconsistency. But the mess and confusion of a functional democracy are exactly its great strength, more people thinking. All other political setups explicitly seek to stop thinking. That is why they sometimes appear clean and efficient. Intelligence is a state of motion, the opposite of keeping everything the same. Creativity always has an element of disorder, whether in one mind or that of many. Democracy is beautiful because it is active, alive and intelligent and deserves respect for it.

A widespread improvement in moral behavior is a necessary part of the success of capitalism and democracy. This is a long, slow process, as individuals gain new freedoms and learn from them. Increasing morality means people thinking more, not less. Progress results in an increase in general activity and the pace of change. Humans are not designed to sit still but to be intelligent. Together our destiny is to wonder and speculate, create and explore, seek truth and solve the riddles of the universe.

The image of humans as entities that exist separate,

alone and inherently in conflict is an insidiously corrosive illusion. Its great attraction is support it lends for comparisons showing one worth more than another. As individual items, there is a scale handy to prove anyone better. Whether best mechanic, politician, musician, cook, mathematician or athlete, a soft cocoon of superiority beckons. Excellence then isolates instead of broadening life. Individual arrogance also decreases intelligence by working against the decentralizing tides of democracy and capitalism. People keep inventing ingenious ways of explaining why they should decide instead of others, why they are smarter and better and so more deserving of the perks and trinkets of life. But if theft is legitimate, then intelligence is not.

The most fundamental fact of human life is that we evolved to maximize the intelligence of the human information system as a whole. We have never existed separate and alone but as intricately connected parts of that system, within which we live our lives. Individual intelligence was worthwhile and increased only in ways which complemented our source of power. People do not exist on a linear scale from stupid to smart. They live in many dimensions, their value to the whole being that they are different. Supermen and philosopher kings do not exist. If they did our world would be much less intelligent.

Hatred is not about the victim, instead a category error in someone's mind, a voluntary severing of connection, a denial of the fact that all humans are intrinsically interconnected. People invent all kinds of ways to cut themselves off. Walking around measuring, categorizing and belittling others may seem a purely private obsession. But the artificial separation it creates decreases intelligence, just like lying, cheating, hurting and stealing. Even when they feel justified by real injury, those who come to hate always lose. Severing connections isolates each of us when we make this mistake from the millions of ways we are naturally linked to others with inti-

16

macy, substance and meaning. It is a personal failure to grasp the largeness of life. All forms of hatred are self-banishments from the community of life, alienation from the essence of the greatest intelligence ever to arise.

True intelligence is found not in any one person. It is the unexpected found in pieces everywhere, in every pair of eyes. Fulfillment in life is not a destination but a journey always in motion, mixing in with the world around. Love, the closest of connections, is the highest expression of intelligence, of our state of nature.

For little round billiard balls, equality is being the same and freedom to roll around is increased by taking others off the table. Since humans are not little balls but information entities, the exact opposite is true. Equality is being different and freedom is radically reduced by taking others off the table. People are equal in that each one is an element of the larger thinking system and all are needed to maximize its intelligence. Acts hindering others from thinking detract from the intelligence of everyone. Condescension is always obvious, as the perpetrator very publically makes their own life smaller and cheaper. Their victims resent it, cooperate less, and close off in turn. Rising out of superiority to equality with all those lesser, acceptance to the core of humanity's great gift, the smallness and particularity of self, is the critical door opening to the wider world of intelligence, dignity and beauty. Freedom is the ability to make choices and move around in the vast information landscape of minds and lives. This requires participation in making things work, more giving than receiving. It is because the equality and freedom of individuals as information entities are essential to intelligence that they are inherent in human existence.

Because people are not objects but information entities, they are happiest not when cut off and alone but when their minds are best connected with the world. A drug induced blank smile is not at all what happiness is about.

17

Whether it's baseball, another person, a job or a song they like, as they find fulfillment in their various peculiarities they are happier and their minds are more engaged. As long as they avoid harming others, this raises the intelligence of the human information system. More thinking is going on. Their happiness is the summit of life, peak experience and function, the highest expression of their unique contribution. Individual happiness is the source of collective intelligence. Can't have one without the other.

Fairness within the human information system is much greater than any list of physical items. Because it consists of enabling everyone to think and contribute it is essential to intelligence. No one can do so if starving or sick, ignorant or in chains. Everyone needs help to grow and flourish. Efforts to increase fairness, to better people's lives, are far more than feel good projects. They are for us, not simply for them.

In the clear cold light of morning the choice to live fully and behave in a moral fashion is obvious. People have invented lots of ways to explain why they should be nice to each other. But at root they all come down to individual awakening, opening to the information realities of life. Human beings perceive directly, without any explanation, theory or religion, that they are connected with others and the world. It is obvious in moments when an individual finds themself suddenly enraptured by another person. The illusion of separateness might unconsciously dissolve when encountering a song or a wayward glance, an ingenious machine or a football pass. It is the recognition of informational connection which inspires the look in a lover's eye, the visceral reaction to a baby's cry, the giddy feeling of a moving world when some work of art gets under the skin. Most people do not need complicated reasons to see grossly immoral acts as just plain wrong. Who has not been overwhelmed by the utter cuteness of a little child? Morality becomes self-evident with the experience of recognizing the warmth and light in another's eye, becoming much more than the right thing, the only thing to do.

Within every person lies a field of life full of hidden places, fuzzy feelings, acres of happenings and kittens and food, every corner filled with vastness, fluid motion moment to moment. Each comes with a mix of warm childhood memories, present experience and dreams of the future, all dense with nuance and impressions. Their information field is an extension and enrichment of all others. For anyone, the experience of recognizing this in one person and then another, a friend, neighbor or passerby, expands the boundaries of life. Multiplied by all those in a town, a region, the world, and the human information landscape seems to go on forever. The furthest corners of every mind fuel the most powerful and intelligent entity ever to exist. Its beauty graces all our lives.

Today awareness is spreading throughout the world of the myriad ways that participating in an actively intelligent society elevates every personal life. Individuals have ever more reasons to believe that their own peculiarities are good not bad, that it is alright for them to be more themselves. The variety of things they can do is expanding, with greater freedom, prosperity and people inventing new pursuits. Large organizations are recognized to be more successful when they enlist the minds of their employees instead of having them do only what they are told. The use of math to make it possible for everyone to make decisions is gaining acceptance. Ever more varieties of people are being allowed, enabled and inspired to participate. Democracy is spreading and theft by those who govern is receding. Even those with guns are slowly awakening to the fact that real power comes from intelligence, the secret to which is to be found in the sweetly innocent smile of a child. The modern flowering of the human information system is wonderful, moral and inherently beautiful.

1

Dancing With You

The experience of knowing you
sparked an awakening of vision
lost somewhere along the way
the light in your eye
ignited a journey
through traces found everywhere
peeping round corners
quiet and loud, hidden in plain sight
past and present, forgotten and new
and slowly, piece by piece
informed by the sense of connection
we had become
a rustling, whispering coming together
gathered pace, insistent, increasingly clear
to really love you, because I love you
I had to grow
stretch understanding and vision
embrace a wider world
without which you would not exist.
* * *

Falling in love is
the most intelligent
thing anyone can do
enraptured by a person
place, concept or vision
linking up, becoming
a more intimate element
of the wider human mind
desire and interest propelling
a new opening
activation of individuality
expanded by
reaching out and mingling
refreshed with hitherto unnoticed
details of the world
renewing commitment to life
and motivating moral balance
by really desperately wanting
from the depths of being
to join, care and think more.
* * *

The most beautiful woman in the world
has arms and legs beyond compare
nose and toes perfectly formed
hair and skin silky
her aspect from afar
raises spirits
rough edges from the day
softened by her voice
but it is not skin or hair
or incomparable silhouette
that makes her so special
though they may be
affected some way
by what I really admire
draws me to her
moment by moment
each time exciting
making skin tingle
hairs rising up
down the back of my neck
what I see
in the light in her eye
in her voice, whispered smile
in her very particular awkwardness
swirling deep down
in some center of the universe within her
an information generator
little whirling dynamo
spinning sensibility unique to creation
an entity that meshes
so completely with my own
to remotest corners of my being
with a glance sweeping me away
over and over for a lifetime she is
the most beautiful woman in the world.
* * *

Love does not occur in isolation
its substance
content of our existence
is a fortuitous distillation
of the information superstructure
weaving through reality
binding us together
in shared systems of thought
without which humans are helpless
our revolutionary source of power
a collective intelligence
bound and driven by love
both essential for survival
and the breath of life
discovered anew
in each generation
person by person, you and me
becoming visible, palpable, alive
as each episode of love
opens us to see
its traces in each other
and in strangers' eyes
personal experience
filling life with understanding
that though we are so small
our love for each other
is of earth shattering importance
foundation
of the greatest intelligence ever to exist
heart of beauty
in the human enterprise

we two born able
to find each other
if we rise up
seize our destiny
embrace our birthright
the default setting is love.
* * *

If I would join with you I must
open doorways to my heart
listening beyond sound and sight
to secrets deep within
hear your feelings
winding softly through inner worlds
and your songs out in open
ringing in my ears
filling all I am
and then
then in morning start again
find a new day's ways to hear
and as days repeat
and I give more
hear more, love more
implications pile up
isolation broken
loses sense
to stay tuned to you
through vicissitudes of fortune
requires courage and strength
to grapple with the ways
your life grows out
encompassing ever wider worlds
for you have no existence all alone
and pathways of involvement
turn out not to be dead ends
opening, listening, giving, loving one
leads to another and another
and out beyond
to kittens and stars and neighbors
for all I open
doorways to my heart
changed forever loving you.
* * *

Indelible impressions
inform all first meetings
floods of data incoming
sights, sounds, smells
and beyond
any list of particulars
a sensing of what's inside
a feeling of presence
a definite who
a brand new wonderment
an expansion of the possibilities of being human
a person
their most important aspects
known in an instant
constant for years
such recognition is common
in everyday life
yet once in a while
intimacy at first sight
totally overwhelms
changing life
as happened
when I met you.
* * *

Love at first sight
any moment, any day
meeting almost anyone
with open heart
awareness of presence
spontaneous arousal
automatic knowing
of a feeling inside
a look in their eye
far beyond
what they're thinking
what they've done
instinctual understanding
of their point of view
empathetic resonation
with a mind's
soft hidden secrets
an ear for the music of their desires
joy of recognition
even tingling skin
a kindred spirit
hello.
* * *

Love is complexity
in the look in your eyes
boundaries collapse
the world opens
crunchier, tastier
visions of beauty entering pores
of mind and feeling
impulses, impressions, new connections
in such overwhelming abundance
that the creeping simplicity of yesterday
belief in straightforward aloneness
comfortable separateness
is only a memory
an illusion of disillusion
self destructive retreat
from glories of reality
that swirl all around
whether witnessed or not
joined in with or not
they awaken in me
every morning I greet you
and tumble anew
falling head over heels
in embrace of a universe
opened to me by you.
* * *

Your thoughts and feelings
dreams and impressions
waves of emotion
the entire intricate
network of information
animating your being
every second every day
the mixed-up moving mystery
informing your smile
beautiful waves your hand describes
things you like and do not
all of that and more
is what is you
what I love so much
though I can never put my finger
on exactly what it is
exactly who you are
except I know for certain
you.
* * *

The substance of love is the same
as the substance of lovers
as whatever makes them them
what they know of themself
what they see in each other
thoughts and dreams
fleeting impressions
overwhelming emotions
passing intuitions
the whole interwoven web
conscious and unconscious
interconnected
flowing together
mingling inextricably
uncountably intricate patterns
with indescribable feelings
of boundaries dissolving
the sweetest elixir
most fulfilling confirmation
of the substance of self.
* * *

How to know
what is real, what pretend
made up feelings, familiar dreams
companions of all waking hours
created by the one most able to deceive
yet imagination comes from somewhere
acts of thought themselves are real
even if/when their truth is not
and cutting clean
through fog and doubt
are moments of pure contact
seconds filled with clearness
sometimes on a mountaintop
or walking slowly down a street
boundaries vanish inside and out
delicious sensations
absolute presence
timeless connection
each time we touch
provides electric awakening proof
you are no illusion
and the whole world is as real
as your existence and mine.
* * *

To get as close as can be
to the purest essence
vital source
wellspring of life
truest reality
intimate touching
most fully in the present
is to open within and without
let passions loose
allow what is inside to rise
with every passing smell, taste, vista
melodious voice drifting round a corner
beauty and love happen
when the tiniest, deepest, innermost
most untouchable thoughts and feelings
mingle their intricate byways
with all the world offers up
denying any
defeats all
so ride the rising storm of complexity
move in balance
get whisper close.
* * *

Something strange can happen
when a bird twitters in a calm blue sky
city sounds muted
all's without stress
an inkling of difference
rises on its own
whispering something new awaits
behind a quiet leaf
or lying on the sidewalk
if I listen carefully
little corners of the world
exponentially expand
opening worlds
bursting with details
from bacteria to distant stars
a hidden cherry I couldn't find
kitty beneath a favorite bush
an overwhelming glimpse
of complexity lurking everywhere
portends maybe
what is normal
what I've missed
not listening.
* * *

Love happens to everyone
without warning they are different
threadbare illusions of separate existence
dissolve in thin air
the experience of uniting
reveals life unjoined
to be an illusion
a trick of remembering
and forever after
that sensation
so immediate, compelling
tactile and irresistible
most intimate glimpse
of the nature of everything
never can go
completely away
though new mornings come
with difficult times
and old fascinations left behind
reminders recur
throughout each day
peeping round corners
staring in the face
tucked in funny little
curves of lips
the ongoing challenge of life
to stay awake
see every moment
the beckoning of reality
love is forever.
* * *

2

Really Touching

Of the wonderment that is you
what do I really know is real?
the fact of thought
does not prove existence
of some outside entity
or separate soul
while such a thing may be
all that's certain is
physical apparatus supporting
an entity of information
the stuff thought consists of
in the right here and now
you are far more beautiful
than any imaginable
pristine, crystallized whatever
more intricate, wonderful
exciting and meaningful
a self-generating thought system
moving and changing
never the same
a dense inner swirl
with tendrils spreading out alive
in every direction you grace with a gaze
and all of it is you, on and on
through my mind, into the garden
memories, dreams, conversations
the trail of connections never ends
winding through all human thought,
encompassing living forms, distant stars
a distillation of the information universe
you embody its grace and beauty
as certain as thought exists.
* * *

If you were not real
your grace an illusion
your smile empty
impulses absurd
laughter sound waves only
your dreams and desires nothing
just figments
if the content of your thoughts
were less real
than mushy grey matter
if your presence were not
of the universe, part of it
a wonderful, natural flowering
of everything that is
if, that is, you did not exist
but you do.
* * *

Could love be
as real as a table or a rock
which when examined closely
are mostly empty space
filled with tiny specks
of energy or strings or something
of mystery dissolving into mystery
compared to such solidity
how substantial could be
the driving force of humanity
flowing active spirit
transforming the planet
a dream, a figment
a reality unto its own
rearranging the cosmos all around.
* * *

You can't have it both ways
no shades of grey exist
love is either real or it's not
if we were only physical beings
using information for our needs
then what seems to join us
would not be real
love reduced
to a pleasant illusion
useful for procreation
yet even though
discounted as artifact
in that picture thought exists
so even in that imaginary
stripped down empty sandy desert
the medium of love
is just as real
as fingers and toes
instead of separate
we are in fact
information beings
using bodies for our needs
what joins us in love
is the essence of reality.
* * *

Physical entities are discrete
information ones are not
a rock is a rock
separate and distinct
no more no less
unlike minds
which reach inside
through imagination landscapes
and back in time
going outside in all directions
invading, including
thoughts and feelings
of people all around
finding commonality
with puppy dog eyes
the outline of a face is softer
than edges of a stone
but what's behind
is nothing of the kind
no firm boundaries
a different order of existence
incomparable dimension of reality
what makes you so special
is both kinds of entity
physical and informational
together, inseparable
allowing our lives to mesh
in mysterious completeness
in this brief moment of time.
* * *

Exactly where
do you begin and I leave off
when we're together or apart
our skin's a boundary of flesh alone
though yours is sweet
so very sweet
when I look at you
your form is not
what I see and feel
and want on foggy nights away
beyond grasping and undefinable
some mysterious beautiful whole
half-glimpsed in morning
not just you but also me
some entity I've never understood
completes the incompleteness
deep within me
makes me feel as though
I with you am one
holding hands
drifting softly through the mist.
* * *

The boundary between us
is ever changing
alive and wild
coming, going
fading in and out
glowing in the dark
sometimes rising to a deafening whisper
in the silence before birds at dawn
it's always there somehow
a nebulous, shifting, evanescent thing
firm, hardy and substantial
though never holdable in hand
it lasts and lasts and lasts and lasts
and I don't know what it is
why and where it comes and goes
all I know is it is not
an emptiness or void
but definitely real, extremely alive
with mysterious ways all its own
it kicks me in the pants
every time I turn and see you coming
dancing through the grass.
* * *

The space in between
has molecules of air
with space in between
no matter how dense
forest trees intertwine
there's always space in between
even when I hold you tightly
space is in between
the discreteness of things
overwhelms with actuality
a blinding rain of particulateness
relentlessly obscuring
the light of human reality
not physical or behaving like particles
shining right through space
no matter how far away you are
between us
there is no space in between.
* * *

Opening to you
allowing inner recesses
to entwine with yours
grow what is me
to become us together
love true, right and real
changes, defines me
restructures my mind
alters the boundary
of inside and outside
new ways of looking
desires to see and hear
reveal our love is not merely
for us alone
the entire menagerie
of people and plants
mountains and creatures
pictures and dreams
all rush in
freshly welcome
as our lives tune afresh
to the world, to life
letting go moment by moment
listening for whispers
even cats can't hear
falling in love with you
is loving all else.
* * *

It is only when I listen
that you appear
an outline in the mist
form emerging
defying confusion
a definitive person
beyond imagination
growing more real
more you
only when
I stop imagining
and listen
listen for you.
* * *

What is it you love
puppy pictures, purple hats
sunny days, an old soundtrack
your own particular mix
of people and places
things happened on
or sought out
each one finding
a home within you
sympathetic pathways in your mind
many preset
others chosen or grown to like
zinnias, mountain sunsets
fuzzy kitties, urban walks
an assortment
of predilections and desires
occurring only once
only in you
intimately connecting
you with the world
and, miraculously, to me.
* * *

So many lights shining
obvious and obscure
multicolored, fuzzy hues
dim and bright facets
of your thoughts and feelings
past and present longings, daydreams
likes and dislikes large and small
hosts of hidden whispers
scraps of songs, forgotten dreams
lingering longings
for friendships unresolved
traces gathered from a lifetime
mingling muttering
in the background
the character and texture
of what is you
let me live warmly in your light
do not extinguish
or allow to fade
in silent encroaching emptiness
any tidbits
trivial or extraneous
momentous or unknown
those swirling sifting fragments
so many fine and fragile
are easily erased, ignored
frittered away in thoughtless loss
evaporating what is special
gift of life for you
and me and humankind

let me savor forever
all the pathways of your mind
for if bit by bit
you let lights dim and flicker out
I am left alone
as slowly, quietly
the you vanishes.
* * *

I love you not because
you're smarter than me
or faster, slower, taller, shorter
musical, math whiz or dunce,
more talkative, sweet smiling
sympathetic, persuasive
hard driving or wayward
straight forward or devious
hard working, slow plodding
quick thinking, methodical
or any category you can think of
for love is larger and greater
than the greatest anyone
than the mostest, the biggest or the bestest
love is precisely that which makes
a mockery of measurement
comparison ridiculous
completely ignoring
being better in any way
than anyone else
that whole way of thinking
vanishes in a flash
every time I think of you.
* * *

You and me in particular
instantly natural
linked automatically
or so it seemed
and then kept on seeming
deeper, more detailed
day after day
year after year
and the mystery of why
never goes away
wrapped in the mystery
that is each of us
of why we are
who we cannot help being
of our sense
of me-ness, of you-ness
the feeling of being
the feeling of you
that I love so much
I'll never know why
but I do.
* * *

From where come fascinations
that fill our lives
the mix that is each person
mystifies them as much
as anyone else
so many preferences
encountered every day
cooking, machinery, travel or football
attraction to one person instead of another
no one gets to choose
which desires
arise naturally
yet smallness and particularity
are not hard to understand
in the larger frame of life
complexity in the world
and in humans within it
is simply intelligence
so grand as to appear
mysterious and unfathomable
from vantage points on the ground
where each must choose
which impulses to pursue and fuel
with desire, drive and love
into the fullness of life.
* * *

Plain as the nose on your face
you're utterly different than me
the way you walk
what delights your eye
tunes you hum
thousands of treasured differences
each a reflection
of imperfection, incompleteness
lack of wholeness
every attribute
merely complementing
all you cannot do
even imagine or hear
and intricacies of thought
you'll never penetrate
but all the many ways
you are incompetent in comparison
with the wonderment of things
natural for this one or that
are for me
exactly the particularities
I love so much
make you greater and grander
day by day
our love together a celebration
of intelligent life.

* * *

So many eyes passing
a wink or hello
or simply meandering
in private worlds
and within behind
the looking eyes
a whole life lies
stretching onward and outward
eons of history
traced over and over
wrapped in new wrinkles
refreshed and reborn
old tales extended
songs reinvented
a world passes by
each new encounter
an overwhelming vastness
that could swallow you whole
oceans of hope mixed with sadness
endless variety and mystery
all related, all connected
senses explode with richness
as you beckon, draw me in
through your eyes.
* * *

A tiny purple being
newborn bit of wrinkly flesh
greets the world with a cry
unviable-seeming infant evokes a first response
of awe at sheer beauty of miraculous fresh life
and then something about the look in its eye
prompts an awareness of strangeness
warm and friendly, welcoming even
but so utterly new and different
right from the start one of a kind
in so many ways that can't be described
more a feeling, instinctual knowing
that this one is unlike any other ever
a miracle of uniqueness
casting fresh light on all gone before
the newborn bears a gift
of awareness and humility
exposing how little anyone has to do
with the most important aspects
of their own mind and feelings
of their own sense of presence
no one gets to choose who they are
only how to deal with their grab bag of particulars
a series of dilemmas imposed by uniqueness
and have sympathy for others
with similar conundrums
and weave all together
create coherence in the echoing vastness
of individuality multiplied
unto billions on earth
and have love for this sweet little one
surprising rebirth
of you and me, of humankind.
* * *

3

With Intelligence and Grace

What difference does
love between us make
a small, peculiar occurrence
in some corner tucked away
lost, unnoticed in the rush
of spinning stars, worlds colliding
insects twitching, chirping birds
and millions and millions of people
milling around
within their worlds
of care and indifference
just the two of us holding hands
joining together moment by moment
make all the difference
in the world.
* * *

How can it be
that this collection of beings
who aren't very smart
so many of whom
write badly
are uncoordinated
incapable of fixing anything mechanical
lack any feeling for poetry
of motion, words or music
can't add or remember facts
even a few who most of the time
seem to be general fuck-ups
how can it be
how does it come about
that such as you
as incredibly small as I
in honest moments know myself to be
how can we be described as intelligent
or insightful or talented
how can such a motley crew
even the best of which in any category
is exposed in light of day
to have huge gaping incompetencies
how can such physical and mental midgets
have risen to inherit the earth?
* * *

The human information system
crafted through the ages
to survive by intelligence
over-endowed with
its primary tool and weapon
as every life form must be
its genius a category leap
rising far beyond
what ever could evolve to be
the smartest, most wily
most dominant individual beast
evolving instead an intelligence
collective in nature
talents not concentrated but disbursed
many sorts of thinking
striving, sometimes clashing
always mingling together
a creative flexibility
revolutionary kind of thinking power
different in function
magnitude, purpose and meaning
than what any single entity could achieve
its elements finely tuned to create with others
each general type essential
every new addition
a welcome extension of the ability and desire
of the entity as a whole to think.
* * *

Everyday life may seem mundane
unimportant in the world
don't be fooled
by the center of the universe
swirling living generator
heartland of intelligence
echo chamber
intricate and vast
mysterious in function
mostly out of sight
spinning thoughts out
of the unknown and unexpected
finding depth and diversity
with inauspicious people
and rising generations
breaking old patterns
even the loftiest
abstract sophisticated concepts
are composed of pieces
rattling around coffee shops
nurseries, football fields
mixing with music
cooking and gardening
every mind taking part
while deciding what to wear
awake to private nuance
each one living
in the thinking of the world.
* * *

Specialists all
particular things
they can do, can't do
do well or only a bit
with good fortune
each one finds a part
only together is anything
good and intelligent made
all need knowledge from the past
and input from parents
teachers and colleagues
adversaries and friends
partners and neighbors
whatever credit one person
may be assigned for contributions
great and small
exceptional and commonplace
each can ever only be
a piece of the puzzle
deserving respect for trying
adding their bit
daring to get
excited about life
and thereby becoming
more fully a part
of the onrushing human thought maelstrom
most intelligent entity in the universe.
* * *

People do so many things I cannot
play music, make machines, cook linguini
mediate disputes, chase footballs
speechify, act in movies
nurture children, fix watches
plot trajectories to the moon
I can't do that
knowing that accomplishments
grow as much from hard work as ability
does little to relieve nagging doubts
that all that I can do and have done
entire collection of a lifetime of thought
is anything more than an invisible drop
in the vast ocean of thinking and doing
it is small consolation that
smallness is everyone's lot
even the greatest, most fantastic
pale to insignificance
their view personal and incomplete
beside the wholeness of thought
of the concert of billions all different
the most intelligent thinking system in the universe
such nebulous abstract premises
come into focus
become real to me
as they do to everyone else
with the knowledge, warmth and certainty
that in one teeny-tiny corner of the world
I've found with you
a part worth playing
beautiful in itself.
* * *

Intelligence begins with love
intimacy is mingling thoughts and feelings
somewhat filling and completing
enormous gaps in understanding
what I can't remember, she does
she loses I find, fix, make,
her choices subtly wiser
when I'm lost at sea
we complement each other
thoroughly, creatively becoming
an entity together
much greater than the sum of two
a wholeness of thought
unattainable alone
intelligence of a higher order
arising out of mixing
tiny fine unnoticed
precursors of decisions
love making intelligence
is depth, meaning, purpose
fulfillment in life.
* * *

Could you and I be
merely two computers
white boxes side by side
unlovely and apart
when switched on
connected in a network
one plus one is a larger one
we fit the pattern at first glance
separate bodies side by side
lovely to some eyes if not others
but as thoughts and feelings mingle
we create and become part of systems
with a higher order of complexity
an ongoing generator of creativity
leaving boxes far behind
an expanse of dreams
impressions, wants, desires
speculations, musings, calculations
infused throughout with the spirit
that is two of us joined
that is millions of thought originators
each different from the start
diverging ever more
as they go their own ways
make life up for their own ends
even as they entwine
matching together
puzzle pieces
wisps of nuance, feeling, being
we are so much more than two
as we weave our minds ever more
into the vastness of intelligence
that is the mind of all people
the highest achievement of life itself
you and I are parts of life
we are alive.
* * *

The default setting is love
primal force of the universe
innocent seeming
simple unpretentious unimportant
source of human power
each person on their own impelled
by very personal feelings
into others' arms
adventures, new ideas
mysteries as well
somehow they just want
to donate free their whimsy
invaluable originality
so absurd on its own
the proud essential element
of a grand intelligence
a role no human can escape
programmed from the start
the default setting is love.
* * *

Struggle in the wilderness
living, dying by the potency
of a revolutionary kind of mind
composed of pieces in a pattern
always arranged the same
impractical musicians, nonathletic priests
groveling politicians
help bring disparate folks together
mechanics fix stoves, clumsy scientists invent
athletes run and hunt
shoppers gather, some cook
others memorize, memorialize the past
all are needed
everyone is known
every voice is heard
as they come together
function as a unit
with failure a constant shadow
cruel outcomes of surviving ensure
only useful kinds of voices endure
ones that hinder or even don't add
drag to mediocrity and destruction
whole groups and parts
resulting over eons
in the most efficiently
creative and intelligent combination
bound by love into a package
of glorious shining beauty.
* * *

Invisible to those who do not see
the greatest secret ever to unfold
magic at the heart of power
in a guise of innocence
a giant stalks the land
terrifying and real
wrecking havoc on all foes who see only
ignominious manifestations
of its presence
each one small, incompetent
so easily defeated, picked up and eaten
yet lions, tigers and bears
are but playthings swatted from the way
by a being from another dimension
transcending former boundaries of the earth
a restless stirring giant of thought
rambling rambunctious playful imagination
incredible revolutionary kind of intelligence
disbursed in millions of tiny parts
heading in disparate separate ways
forged as one by numberless varieties of love
a force so improbable as to render invisible
the face of the giant
conqueror of all who cannot divine
the meaning behind
the sweetly innocent smile of a child.
* * *

Every beast in their domain
master of the universe
by evolution honed razor sharp
far more than good enough
supreme within their niche
through emergencies and hard times
only overqualified survived
descendents magnificent and able
far surpassing everyday necessity
and by far the greatest of them all
is the one that can't be seen
the secret of its power is weakness
innate flaws its source of strength
the essence of the scheme is smallness
its genius incompetence
by themself each part so puny
naked and defenseless
mentally disabled
having given up over eons
ability to think completely
prosper all alone
each one sinking down
to critical extremes of difference
widespread idiosyncrasy
partiality of vision
patterned into standard types
set to function mixed together
a very steep price
necessary to be essential
to the thinking whole

finally giving birth to you
a wonderment of beautiful imperfection
graced with the perfection
of being needed
along with each and every other one
pieces of the grandest most elaborate puzzle
most intelligent and powerful thinking entity
ever to arise.
* * *

Exceptional people are useful indeed
for any one task at hand
but the thinking system all comprise
is far more subtle and complex
than any enumeration of success
in real life the greatest thing
an honest person sees in mirrors
is the amazing
ordinariness of uniqueness
each one gets
just a smattering
from the pool of talents
some of these, a few of those
a peculiar mix of traits
useless all alone
with luck well-suited
for a few tasks in their time
should they find
courage and imagination to engage
recreate the secret
of a package tried and tested
through the utmost extremities
the highest order of intelligence ever to arise
it's most potent attribute
not that some are all-encompassing geniuses
but that none are.
* * *

A good idea
popped into existence
found a new way, solved a problem
though a handful claimed the credit
there is no way
to ever figure out
exactly from where and why it came
composed of strands
reaching far back in the past
through friends and neighbors
over many lands
threads of rhythm, color, rhyme
outrageous mistakes, hallucinations, dreams
distilled from amorphous
shape-shifting bundles of thought
wandering the human landscape
so much seeming useless, frivolous
heading down rat holes, off across horizons
spinning apart, attending private concerns
with occasions of coalescence
development, discovery, invention
of anything useful or interesting
only the most obvious sign
that what can appear to be a mess
of incoherence, disunity, pettiness and sloth
is the face of creativity and power
the most intelligent entity in the universe.
* * *

Knowledge stream
flowing through time
all live within it
partaking, contributing
singing along
creating eddies
standing in the way
splashing and swimming
unable even to imagine
escape from context
forever seeking fulfillment
in greater immersion.
* * *

Scenes of other people
fill all waking hours and dreams
relationships, impressions
faces, songs, hopes and fears
good and bad, like, dislike
not to be denied
can't be gotten out of mind
obsession's normal
indifference anomaly
autism disorder
getting closer
sensors turn on
automatically ignite
crazy love for one in particular
illuminates with blinding force
the defining feature of humankind
a giant tide of mania
pervades the vast parade
pushing limits of control
but even when destructive
twisted to perversion
no matter what transpires
everyday fixation
stands as testament
the default setting is love.
* * *

It simply isn't true
that your happiness
matters naught but to you
maintain its pursuit
develop all
its finer curlicues
of pleasure and fulfillment
and as you feel better
more at one with a world
you make your own
as you go more and more
the way that only you can go
so my life becomes enhanced
more intelligent
in breadth and detail
more beautiful
as you grow the things you love
for our lives are entwined
your thoughts are mine.
* * *

Happiness is
the summit of life
peak experience and function
engaged most fully
with the many things you love
all those little nuances
fine texture of individuality
alive and tingling
thinking, feeling, doing
make the world brighter
open up, stand up
feel better in yourself
not just for you
and a few others close around
but for all in circles
spreading ever wider
your happiness
is the highest expression
of your unique contribution
to the intelligence of the whole
your willingness and enthusiasm
inspires others
as well as me.

* * *

Inseparable twins
conjoined at the heart
individual happiness
collective intelligence
can't have one
without the other
happiness the active state
of thinking the most
intelligence rising
when more people think more
creating and getting along
in the age-old dance of human life
an unstable, ever moving
critical balance
burden of everyone
shared by you and me
working things out
finding joy
in each other's work and play.
* * *

Feel good about yourself
for all the things you love
with pleasure pursue happiness
enliven your small slice of life
know that doing so grows beauty
for me and others
the field we live in
is richer, more intelligent
as your life
flowers ever fuller
even things you tell no one
private comforts
secret thoughts
find connection
within you
through you
the joy in your smile
warms the world
whose common purpose
source of intelligence and fulfillment
are realized
in your happiness.
* * *

A simple smile passed along
lifts if only for a while
some random lonely aching heart
and just that single tiny spark
lights them up enough
to turn around and send some cheer
a welcome, happy glance
to a passing neighbor, stranger, friend
and so it goes over and over, on and on
rippling through the vast expanse
of person after person
flitting quickly
traipsing lightly
over mind after absent mind
emotion's valleys
ecstatic heights
stretching way out past horizons
crossing borders, on through
cities, farms and continents
round and round til finally
the impact of the wave
inspires you to shine
your special smile on me.
* * *

4

Through Wild Fields

More free than birds by far
for all they can do is fly
follow instinct to survive
far better human life
vaster playing fields than sky
movement, choice, opportunity
new directions beckon
with imagination, memory
dreaming, planning, wondering
wandering in a passing smile
picked up suddenly by a song
new sports to play
mysteries unravel
cities explore
at every turn
decisions are freedom
whether to engage
let others play
the allure of life
ever fuller, freer
brings me outside with you
in the garden's enfolding silence
watching swallows whirl in unison
across the evening sky.
* * *

Freedom is not
living alone in a wilderness
humans never did that
don't come from that
not designed for that
freedom is a way
of living with other people
actively immersed
in the thinking machine
in which everyone takes part
whether they like it or not
know it or not
on the field
of freedom's potential
of plans and dreams
where decisions play out
each gets to choose
over and over
whether to help the field flourish
grow dense and inclusive
more intricate and complex
opening opportunity
for themself and all others
to live life more fully
shoulder responsibility
contribute and take part
in the great power and beauty
in which it is such a privilege to live.
* * *

Freedom is belonging
much more and harder
than simply making choices
even the most personal
preferences and attractions
flourish in gardens
not alone
separation
solitary confinement
is opposite of free
moving around within
the information landscape
of minds and lives
requires involvement
more giving than receiving
participation
making things work
in ways expanding
the field of life
plunging in, committing all
following imagination
searching for, inventing
the great rewards of life
connections heartfelt and true
freedom is giving love
to you.
* * *

Information fields
patterns and texture
memories and dreams
smiles and frowns
everywhere you go
everyone you meet
everything you think
all life's playground
is the field of freedom.

Characters large and small
street sweeper ladies in orange vests
pinstripes with sneakers
work boots and pointy heels
the self-righteous, stubbornly honest
schemers, dreamers, path followers
it takes all kinds
to make the world dance
across the field of freedom.

Lost in a dream
repeating scenarios
righting the past
caressing self image
is no way to live
bored by stagnation
gasping for air
break out to daylight
on the field of freedom.

Lawyers' bickering
sideshows grow
as ever more voices
are allowed to rise
their options multiplied
by figuring out how
to keep the peace
all live better expanding
the field of freedom.

Freedom and equality
twin halves of one thing
people are equal
in their right to be free
unchained only
when living together
sharing a field of freedom.

You and I together
all alone is not enough
for our lives to flourish
for our love to grow
we must live in a world
expanding and growing
creating new fields of freedom.
* * *

Peace is a state of motion
war stagnation
breaking of ties
interruption of love
reduction to simplicity
humans alive
have minds always moving
ferment is their state of nature
most active and productive
individually fulfilling
increasing complexity
as long as they get along
it all can seem
so frivolous and useless
merely personal happiness
sports, gardens, cars and beer
yet step back and watch
the beauty of intelligence
unfolds in unassuming attire
varied infatuations of daily life
propel all levels
of the most intelligent thinking entity
ever to exist
leavening with variety, depth and strength
bestowing purpose filled with love
all occurring only once
rising, changing through the day
peace for humans
is the drama of freedom
intelligence is a state of motion.
* * *

Little round billiard balls
equality is being the same
freedom to roll around increased
by taking others off the table
humans are not like balls
equality is being different
freedom radically reduced
by taking others off the table
increased only
by active involvement
embracing all others
ever more fully
in the field of life
so different in kind
people and balls
so thankful I am
that millions each unique
grow the space
I'm free to bounce around in
that as I join you in a hug
you're so unlike me
sharing equality with you
is freedom.
* * *

You and me
though I'm twice your size
we are equal
in the vast reach of life
each a consciousness
appearing for a short while
experiencing in our own way
the mystery of uniqueness
with a presence
ways of feeling
predilections great and small
extremely partial points of view
that need each other
to make wholeness
out of thought, of life
having purpose
finding meaning
only as essential elements
of the human thinking system
in which love is real
when I rise
to equality with you.
* * *

Living with you elevates my life
not by the list of attributes I admire
but by living with one
so utterly different
the ongoing adventure
of trying to be your equal
sets me free
from imaginary straitjackets
illusions of separation
opening to you
clears access
to the immediate present
releasing unforeseen impulses
from uncharted recesses
of body and mind
ridiculous and pertinent
coarse and fine
free to rise and play unburdened
dancing with you through fields of life.
* * *

Rise to the freedom of equality
beyond greater and lesser
move through life
increasing intelligence
associating with everyone
all kinds and abilities
even those who disagree
have something to add
strangers just sitting there
expand possibilities
explorable if not excluded
without them life shrinks
into illusions of self-worth
inflated by incessant measurement
heartless traps filling life
with endless boring litanies
less than one, more than another
gaining self-esteem
while losing the world
turn away, spurn temptation
choose intelligence, fuller life
the highest status in the universe
equal with all humankind.
* * *

Ideas, scraps of thought
feelings, songs, visions
hurt and hope
flit around the world
altered and renewed
at every turn
popping into view
brought in focus
with inimitable aplomb
every moment every day
never completely owned
by anyone alone
though each is due
full credit for rising up
taking responsibility
for their part
their thoughts and actions
contributions
to the ongoing saga
of their life
of the life of all.
* * *

When all are equal
thoughts can rise
beyond levels
possible for any one
what's thought about
becomes more important
than who thought it
truth unstuck
from sticky ownership
is free to find its way
among varieties of nuance
in fluid fields of consciousness
across which all can dance
along the path
of treating others right
free at last
to find their own way
optimizing uniqueness
creating in their own
instant of time
the highest form of intelligence
ever to arise
happening when all desire
to live their own life
in that precious balance
free and equal.
* * *

There is no one else
all decisions great and small
rest on ordinary shoulders
with private, narrow focus
all so insignificant seeming
another grain of sand
in the sweep of history
but their decisions
are not petty but grand
courageous for being both
small and essential
the genius
of the decision-making whirlwind
overtaking the universe
is reliance on each one
propelled by love of life
to add their unique
tentative piece to the puzzle
evolving the increasing complexity
of a more moral and intelligent world.
* * *

Chew gum and walk
at the same time
serve others, make money
all who take initiative
must do both at once
at the mercy of others
who take it or leave it
money is math
measuring tool for deciding
which one is wanted
and how much can be done
daily life has hard choices
scarce resources
everything always
takes longer, costs more
no one's paid as much
as they think they should
so those who would make
some new thing really happen
disciplined by having
to make it add up
need to find ways of caring
about the people involved
really deep down wanting
them to be happy
is the greatest secret
vital ingredient
in figuring precisely how
to fill their desires
in ways that don't cost too much
serve to make money
make money to serve
chew gum and walk.
* * *

Through the faulty lens
of obsession with power
other forms of thought
seem of lesser consequence
like those pursued by me and you
it's so much fun to deride
types of thinking
unconcerned with status
some traditionally women's concerns
cooking, shopping, fashion, kids
as well as so-called male pursuits
sports are for dummies
mechanics are troglodytes
perseverance through hard labor
or concentration on math
though intricate and difficult
contributions to the whole of thought
essential to prosperity, intrinsically interesting
are not about
being better or above
but the destiny and purpose of humankind
is a higher order of complexity than dominance
a form of intelligence
maximized by love
to include all forms of thought
power like others is needed
but corrupts the love
that makes the world go round
so must be, forcibly at times,
kept in perspective.
* * *

Down through the ages
those in control
claim fairness as excuse
echoing old slogans
a place for everyone and everyone in their place
we think and you do and we'll take care of you
but absolute fairness is stasis
bereft of creativity, initiative
missing the point of life
visions of everyone
nicely quiet and in order
are nightmares not dreams
horror not paradise
their imposition resulting
in police states and mass murder
for they directly contravene
the most fundamental human reality
our destiny is to think
even now sirens tout
idylls of peace and fairness
dispensed by nice philosopher kings
like my neighbor next door
but no thank you, not for me
I'd rather fly free and make a mess
contribute if I can
help others think free, make mistakes
only together can any rise up
displace obedience with initiative
ignite creative excitement
take responsibility for complexity
push life in new directions
splash puddles of complacency
over and over restart
the vast human engine of thought

fueled by the kind of fairness
found in freedom
each and every
somewhat incompetent individual
enabled, allowed and inspired
to undertake ever more
decisions in their lives.
* * *

The simplest of visions
drives modern life forward
the American Dream
proclaims it's good and important
for everyone to make decisions
including even you and me
but for those who are so much better
think thoughts of little people inconsequential
the dream is nonsensical
its message invisible, reduced to its symbols
prosperity, refrigerators, guns and cars
such shallow arrogance is blind
to the revolution of our time
the proposition
of freedom for all
provides personal motivation
and general justification
to force open
the most difficult and critical
impediment to human potential
institutional, philosophical
viscerally emotional objections
to getting little voices raised and heard
the shy, odd, peculiar and strange
rebellious and those that sound the same
voices small and lonely
the less talented and nonpolitical
equipping them with a vision
of largeness and complexity
morality and intelligence
unleashing magic innate
to the collective human mind

a way that inspires all
to think and wish others the same
will always be a dream
for it's not an end state
not about perfection
instead on purpose
unleashing imperfection
intelligence is by nature
moving and changing
needing improvement forever
the dream is a bright star leading the way.
* * *

Dog bites man isn't news
man bites dog is
hidden in the news is humor
a morning paper lightens the day
in addition to sports and comics
a few stunts and disasters
some cops and robbers
and cute pictures of people and kittens
grave events are managed
by a wild cast
of mostly well meaning characters
forever tripping over
amazing personal flaws
and gaps in knowledge
playing roles as pompous pontificators
joining a three-ring circus
of miscellaneous clowns
who make the news
by shouting on and on about
the supreme importance of arguments
about absolutely nothing
twisting real life into cartoons
of imagined and fabricated differences
as humor it's bittersweet
yet sometimes
if you look hard enough to see
baby steps of progress emerge
from the messiness of ongoing affairs
the ever swirling confusing chaos
of the human comedy
the divine comedy
* * *

Freedom on a large scale
finds realization in daily life
through decentralizing decision making
the practical beauty
of more thinking going on
in every corner minds mixing
in intimate dance
unleashing incompetence
flip side of variety
source of productivity
messy, disruptive swirls of activity
viewed with dismay
by those opposed to intelligence
welcomed by those willing
to shoulder responsibility
guided by the light
of endless possibilities
facilitated by belief
in a moral center
to which most
gravitate over time
freedom works
intelligence is beautiful
because the default setting is love.
* * *

Freedom world wide
the revolution of our era
more and more people
all kinds everywhere
allowed, encouraged, enabled, inspired
to make ever more decisions in their lives
a time of excitement and promise
rapid increase
of intelligence and morality
a fulfillment of destiny
more thinking going on
as people learn ways to get along
together our purpose is
to wonder and speculate, create and explore
seek truth and solve the riddles of the universe.
* * *

5

See Clearly

I like to watch her figure things out
softly weigh fresh pathways
through daily life
finding her own ways
to make things better
with personal touches
whimsical choices
expressing thereby
unique sensibility
daring to expose
private patterns
innermost desires
letting come out
gifts to the world
in watching her decide
I see her
entranced
I wonder how
to enable, facilitate
keep the magic flowing
allow her beauty to blossom.
* * *

Sometimes disconnected
world gone cold
all smiles frozen
reaching out cannot touch
fingers get only almost there
a feeling of being
absolutely alone
seems suddenly, creepily certain
but I am the luckiest guy in the world
having your touch to wake me up
an electric connection
thrills my skin
turns my attention
to the depths of your smile
where the way back to realness
shines into my eyes
showing me that I am
like all humans wired
to touch everything
find beauty
in lonely pairs of eyes
connections are everywhere
disconnection is illusion
the default setting is love.
* * *

Unexpected moments
cast away illusion
opening the world
it could be the look in a lover's eye
some scrap of forgotten song
or magic in a beautiful football pass
what a second before seemed
overwhelming loneliness
vanishes
absorbed in compelling cuteness
of a kitten or little child
drawn into drama
of friends and neighbors
dreams, emotions, ideas
the information milieu
in which all live
beckons with enticing confections
offering up thousands
of little favors and delights
tasty samplings of universal truths
invitations to live
more wholeheartedly every day
relax, let the world wash over
rise up, play a part, do the right thing
for the intermingling going on all around
is real, is important, is life itself,
is your life and mine.
* * *

To an originator of thoughts
the information they consist of
can come to seem
isolated and tied
content of mind
just a useful tool
a function of machinery
an episode of it
servant to its needs
hard reality reduced
to nothing more
than perpetuating
flesh and blood
getting exactly backwards
natural history, causation and experience
the machinery is the tool
of the life code inside
each awakening consciousness
a perpetuation of
the human information system
without which creation
would not have been possible
of the delicate, intricate beautiful being
that is you.
* * *

So much of the world
that other critters see and sense
I cannot
colors, infrared to ultraviolet
motion beyond a limited range
magnetism
dense detail of sounds and smells
how much more intricate must appear
tree leaves rustling in the breeze
with increased shutter speed
of cat or dog eyes
but I have something they do not .
through a magic doorway
I can know and feel and see and sense
all those worlds and so much more
right in front of me
in air between my fingers
and way out through space
dimensions transcending space and time
all accessed through information fields
the dimension which unlocks the rest
within which whole worlds of delights
can be sought and found
including my favorite.
* * *

Look out a window
see information landscapes all around
pattern, structure, form
everywhere in everything
simple as shapes of stones and stars
clear as the note of a distant horn
compelling as a child's whisper
amazing beauty for all who see more
than particles, not solid anyway
waves of energy, whatever that is
for the information carried by them
is intrinsic to, inseparable from them
always everywhere woven
into the original fabric of existence.

Look out a window
information sides of things
rise powerfully out of shadows
rearranging particles and forces
changing shapes of everything
information entities
perpetuate themselves
mutate, progressively experiment
luxuriate in creativity
life forms
ever more complicated and varied
rise out of the vast sea of information
woven into the original fabric of reality.

Open a window for a breath of fresh air
the landscape gives
a shock to all senses
sights sounds smells
carry multilevel messages
rushing in overflowing
aware and unaware
regions of the mind.

See information
in every aspect
of all things physical
flowers, rocks, air in between
imbued with the same stuff
as imagination
so looking out is the same
as mingling with.

Look out a window
at information landscapes
in eyes of people walking by
next door neighbors, forgotten friends
filled with dreams, emotions, stories
each a vast field
inviting exploration, participation
accept the challenge to stay open
to the windows of their eyes.

Inside your window
lives a landscape
of thoughts and feelings
tiny hidden nooks of whispers
moving menagerie of information
swirling together
forming a consciousness
able to reach
within the window and without.

See windows opening
information landscapes outside and in
have boundaries of connection
not separation
what's outside comes in
insides spill out
windows are open
information flows across sills
continuously mingling, rebuilding
providing the part that can act
with an ever wider more intelligent
field of information
for thoughts and feelings to rumble around
touching, smelling, looking, joining
creating, rehashing, growing and deepening
opening to the inside happens fully only
with opening to the outside
mixing together, the entire collection
springs into action
barreling along through life.

Look out a window
you are not alone
never have been, cannot be
humans form an information system
reliant on inclusion and inspiration
of small and fragile
imperfect individuals
to grow and join together
as the most intelligent
creative and powerful entity ever to exist
integrated into the information landscape
of the universe at large.

Looking out our window
you and me alive
together with each other
and the world beyond
the greater mixing lending
context, depth and meaning
to the love that enables
the human mental system
to dominate existence
with warmth and beauty
always beginning again
as we live in love
dancing real and forever
across the information landscape.
* * *

Information can seem so bloodless
as do matter, energy, space and time
with which it comes packaged
for it is like them
a hard fact
but the one that
gives life to the rest
just look around
information landscapes everywhere
embedded as structure of rocks and wind
dancing in a million wavelets in the sun
growing into life form after form
staring back through
cat's slow blinking eyes
watching every watcher
who by witnessing takes part
necessarily belonging
adding thinking
seeing, feeling, blinking
to the rocks and wind
and quiet smiling faces
walking by.
* * *

That teeniest tiniest
most reduced to its essence
central originating point within you
the real you
whatever else it may be
in the right here and now
consists of information
pure and simple
the source of all thoughts is thoughts
feelings deep down are feelings
however much patterns may be
ultimately embedded
in neurons or ether
or suspended in thin air
matters not
information is what moves within
as you move within
the information landscape
where all life, your life is home.
* * *

Whatever other worlds
may lie beyond
in this one here and now
the phenomenon of consciousness
thoughts and feelings, impulse, desire
abstract speculation and hidden drives
inside, outside
the very living center of I
is information through and through
and since the properties and patterns
of that omnipresent essence
are the driving force and substance
of all life forms
it's in the warm hard firmness
of the real world
that our love exists
grows and flourishes
where we mingle inextricably
the essence of our lives
everything central
everything frivolous
everything mine is yours.
* * *

Throughout the ages
answers have arisen
enabling all to grasp
information realities
fundamental to their lives
though cluttered with ancient science
and extraneous do's and don'ts
beneath window dressings
of myth and paraphernalia
religions express insight essential
for navigating the human enterprise
belief in spiritual worlds
renders palpable
the informational essence of life
illuminating the utter reality
of the love and intimate connections
with others and the world
that are the earthly substance
of every human life
alternative visions of hate
of random, senseless lives of separation
nasty, brutish and short
are simply incorrect.
* * *

Time spent
doing and discovering
solving, mediating, struggling
with varied aspects of life
connects as surely as
a meditating yogi
or chanting priest
with the wonderment
that fills the universe
for reality is constantly moving
changing, destroying, creating
and to participate
swim with the current
or against
create or affect
some little eddy
in the passing tide
is a connection
a fulfillment
an involvement
every bit as much as
merely listening.

* * *

Peak experience
intense, focused concentration
sudden whirlwind sweeps all
up into the sky
every scrap of consciousness
wrapped up with a place, a smell
thousand details of a smile
all else ceasing to exist
right there and then is all that is
wonderful, exhilarating
but frightening too
for complete absence
of past and future
of sense of self
don't turn away
whether new face or old
a bird's flight, a song
or a mountaintop view
whatever wraps you up in itself
rise up join in
treasure love that finds you
all life can be
a peak experience.
* * *

Something about that sensation
of complete connection
can't be ignored or forgotten
captures attention
puts in new perspective
all life before and after
it could rise unbidden
on a hilltop all alone
or unlooked for
in a fog of snowflakes
catching glimmers in your eye
a thrill runs down the spine
freezing for an instant
time and thought
posing once again
the question haunting
every new experience
am I able
can I rise up
summon willingness
strength, honesty, resolve
to meet the promise I have seen
appearing unexpected
over and over again
embrace the challenge of everyday life
connect fully with myself
with you, with life, with the day.
* * *

The mystery of being is everywhere
feel it tingling right at fingertips
something more than meets the eye
infinite sensations
unknowable depths
grace every surface as well as air
absolute presence can be felt
so immediate every moment
yet if somehow
your feel for life gets lost
slipping out of sight
vanishing in silence
reach out once more
even with conscious
thinking sides of mind
follow threads of information
connections weaving consciousness
into patterns with all else
keep aware, keep awake
listening with all senses
whispers of eternity beckon
intimations of certainty
that you yourself
and all others too
are special sprouts of life
concentrated distillations of the universe.
* * *

6

Sunshine

New meaning is given to our love
by belief in the reality of information
automatic feelings of warmth are nice
surges of desire have their place
but experiences of love gain power
to change all trajectories of life
when unchained, let loose
by conscious awareness
that they are high expressions
essential links
in a grand universal enterprise
the prototype for all other relations
friend or foe, in business or fun
nothing matters more than enveloping all
in warm currents of love
which I feel first and most for you.
* * *

Somehow it seems just natural
to treat her right
look for ways to make her happy
filling gaps in a mind
deeply flawed
so differently than mine
not just to get her help
ameliorating
complementary incompetencies
with which I'm riddled
something inside
is simply possessed with desire
to make sense of confusion
build coherence from chaos
make more whole
our small corner of the world
follow that upwelling of feeling
always rising in her direction
filling with reality and conviction
the vision that we function as one
we are one
we are life.
* * *

Just as I love watching you
exploring, finding, deciding
so must I look with a favorable eye
on the doings of so many
I know little or not at all
for your life to be free
you need a welcoming world
offering opportunity and support
and just as I delight
in the spark in your eye
as you wend your way through life
so must I look to find the same
in every pair of eyes
for the essence of mind
its context, meaning, importance
is for everyone
everywhere the same
closing my eyes to them
would be shutting off communion
with thought itself
with all I love most about
the one I love the most.
* * *

Within her eyes
I saw a field of life
full of hidden places
fuzzy feelings
places long forgotten
acres of happenings and kittens and food
fluid motion moment to moment
every corner filled with vastness
and then
I saw right next to her
another pair of eyes
windows opening to the breeze
and then
another pair, another
they would not stop passing by
within each face another world
exploding living color
in the moment that I looked
and every time I tried to fix my gaze
upon a favorite spot
find some firmness
point of reference
certainty dissolved
in all directions
as further mazes beckoned
richly dense with
nuance, impressions, memories
and my comforting world
of hierarchy, measured identity
certainty and order
faded away
replaced with wonderment.
* * *

Names for love
trace connections
strong and weak
subtle and obvious
family, friendship
interests, fascinations
duty, sacrifice
responsibility, fairness
a wide variety of relations
wrapped in emotion
the fields of opportunity
on which life is played
neither means to ends
nor debts to be paid
not trivial or absurd
not cast off lightly
all pertain to you
and George and Harry
(I don't know Harry)
any approximately accurate view
of the human facts of life
understands morality as the basis
of the intelligence of all
linking minds together with
intimacy, substance and meaning
when joined with vision
recognizing warmth and light
in every passing stranger's eyes
it becomes self-evident
much more than the right thing
the only thing to do
the force of human destiny
begins right here now
with me and you.
* * *

Everything matters
everything you do or say
where you go
what you do
all the secret hidden thoughts
passions, fears, hopes and dreams
good or bad
happy or sad
adding, subtracting
building or breaking
it all exists
as part of you, of me
of the flowing thoughts
of humankind
your life and mine
happen only once
a single chance every moment
to be alive
right now and forever.
* * *

Join in laughter
incompetence is everywhere
silly and incongruous
laugh not to show
anyone better or worse
play instead with the natural fate
facing each and every one
all ability
to contribute to intelligence
stems from having
a partial and quirky
character of mind
never more
than an incomplete grasp
of what's going on
yet possessed with vision to imagine
a wholeness beyond
making silly mistakes
over and over falling victim
to circumstances
awkward and ridiculous
this universal contradiction
of aspiration and individuality
is the source of laughter
essence of funny
so laugh to say
we're all in it together
creating incredible intelligence
requires individual pratfalls
join in, reaffirm
instead of war
let's live intimately together
with laughter and with fun.
* * *

Make a mark for destiny
make a mark for love
all alone neither prospers
ending up in empty clouds
in balance each gives
guidance to the other
enabling goals, building fullness
it was fortune that I met you
spark of love lit up our lives
we set out on a course together
held on tight
through mishap and success
out of all accomplishments
experiences of a lifetime
the hardest and the proudest is
we did it all with love.
* * *

How to know what's right and wrong
when rules no longer make much sense
when new vicissitudes intrude
unpredicted quandaries
bad alternatives
uncertain outcomes
degenerate into confusion
hold on fast
never forget
the twin roots of morality
maximize intelligence
of all involved
with all involved
and look for the way
that simply feels right
with love for one, with love for all.
* * *

A neighbor of mine long ago
smoked a pipe
puttered in his garden
was pleasant passing conversation in the street
little I knew of his other lives
exact nature of his passions, job, kids
didn't really matter
nor did disagreements
he was simply fine by me
we two a small society
occasional meetings giving each a lift
joining the cacophonous
urban background hum
its' enormous assortment of folks
living and thinking together
through each other adding to it all
tiny scraps of thought
and the warmth of friendship
and just by maintaining
that private balance of peace
forgiving and allowing
each other some space
we created a ripple
of love and peace spreading out
our gift to the world.
* * *

Make it beautiful
make it sweet
in harmony
with materials and surroundings
make it so it
functions smoothly
to ends you have imagined
make it sing of love
to participants and passersby
and out beyond horizons
take pride in work
in craftsmanship
best you can
do all things well
gifts to the world
make beautiful
your life and mine.
* * *

The song from which they all derive
most primal chant
hypnotic rhythm
filling every corner
lasting throughout ages
if it really moves the heart in time
must be a song of love.

Listening purely to the notes
hear a song within
music is no longer noise
when magic's wrapped inside
sounds that tingle under skin
raising secret passions
sing in tune with all life's rhythmic
secret song of love.

Love songs sing about much more
than any one romance
hope in one life multiplies
ripples spreading far
love sincere inspires in others
meaning, interest, hope
and love of life.

Far from being trivial
harmonies of youth
merely for the purpose
of facilitating babies
love songs touch the heart of life
tie together all its threads
making sense of randomness
foundation of intelligence
sweet melody of morality.

Sing a song of living free
simple, true and joyful
find your song, be yourself
celebrate engagement
join as many as you can
in every way
that suits your heart
keep singing songs of love.
* * *

Lies big and little
black and white, glaring, subtle
create distance
between people
breaking lines
of thought and feeling
reducing almost always
intelligence all around
but it's often hard to figure out
in the flow and stress of life
whether in the end
though all are dangerous
which are hurtful
which are not
in friendship's fragile fabric
even little holes can spread
and lies we whisper
to ourselves on lonely nights
can rot the inner strands
of bonds of trust so carefully built
the most that can be promised
is best efforts and intent
my life is bound with yours
closeness wrapped
in honesty.
* * *

7

Wind and Rain

Servants through the ages have known
not all who are above condescend
and treating others badly
is not about the victim
yet such knowledge never wholly staunches
pain of sleights
those knowing smirks, casual dismissals
over-simple explanations
discretely sophisticated sneers
and that glance
passing in the street
a silent scream of horror
at how painful it can be
to say hello to those below
which is everyone
sooner or later
recipients of trivial degradation
face the challenge of transcending hurt
of not returning like with like
maintaining balanced vision
seeing majesty
in the fact that
everyone is flawed
letting love arise at every meeting
recognizing vistas
extensions of human beauty
behind every pair of eyes
finding respect even for those
who cannot escape
the intoxicating tyranny
addictive abyss
of being better.
* * *

Such an annoyance
inconvenient others
get in the way, muddle things up
need to be helped and compensated for
so often a hindrance to what's going on
from private lives to large affairs
it seems cleaner, efficient and makes you feel better
disregarding, excluding, discarding
the useless, unbeautiful, ignorant and dumb
skip down the path
there's no need to regret
opportunities forgone
what never takes place is easily forgot
as are all the boring, useless and lame
the no longer present
the endless procession of half-baked personas
incomplete, incompetent, self-centered and weak
it's because of all them
that the world's such a mess
life stuck forever in round after round
of meaningless spinning wheel emptiness
all by yourself
it's so much more pleasant to imagine
you are perfect.
* * *

Hatred is not about the victim
instead a category error
inside perpetrators' minds
all of us one time or another
come to see some other
as not one of us
so logical, normal and ordinary seeming
there may be dastardly deeds, inferior nature
wrong ideas, hostile intentions
hurt and heat of insult and injury
or resentment of difference
those higher, lower or out of place
or some myth defining as evil
the variety and spontaneity of life
or simply joining with crowds
in current fashions of exclusion
so many complications
so many ways to cloud vision
obscure beauty
and little by little
lights go out
as slice by slice
this person, that group
pieces of the world
get banished from
the accepted community of life
inflicting creeping punishment
on those who build themselves
walls ever higher
lives ever shallower
ever smaller, more constricted
prisons of imagination
lasting even for a lifetime
as life outside rushes on.
* * *

Those who hate don't think they do
just basically decent
reacting best they can to facts
some other folks are not so nice
incompetent, stupid, consumed with vice
and then by so correctly thinking
such very important thoughts
as if by magic
a feeling of goodness warms the heart
for after all they are not the one
with this particular fault or that
did not do those odious things
they are not the one
and slowly, piece by piece
seduction becomes complete
alienation from the essence
of the greatest intelligence ever to arise
within which egregious faults
instead of bad
are sources of opportunity
and even those who cover their tracks
by repeating litanies of other's faults
even those possessed
by conceptions of hate
are in fact
persons inside
able as are all to open up
to beauty and connection
there to be found
in every pair of eyes
every pair of eyes.
* * *

A plague of throw-off comments
disparaging motives unknowable
they're only in it for themselves
he tried to run me down
strangers are all mean and cheap
insincere, malevolent
unidimensional
not like you and me
everyday trivia
with an enormous price
the poison seeps forward
raising hackles in its objects
who know what's going on
and perniciously backward
making denigrators feel good
negatively self-identified
as more moral and superior
for not being them
shrinking the territory
of their own slice of life
infecting themselves with hate
all for a commonplace mistake
dearth of imagination
an unwillingness to see
bright light shining
in a random pair of eyes.
* * *

Every act of condescension puts
shallowness of the condescendor
on flagrant display
affording objects of their contempt
intimate views right up their ass
an emptiness inside
denial of life, of love
pressuring them to lash out
with those nasty smirks
airs of superiority
having nothing at all to do
with who is being condescended to
offenders are even often
completely unaware
engrossed in chasing after
ever higher associations
aspirational trappings
the right art, correct thought
beautiful people
in constant lifelong effort
to elevate themself
above all the rest of us
their hate is absent minded
not about the victims
who always know it's there
so even though it always hurts
slough it off, smile in good cheer
the poor sufferer
just might maybe someday
grow a little
accept their own incapacities
as making them larger not smaller
and so be relieved
of the pressing urge to smirk.
* * *

Early pressure to measure up
can scar the vulnerable for life
you can be anything
ridiculous in its face
maestro, scientist, whatever
just climb somehow high enough
who you are is what's important
cling to whatever plateau
you can attain
identity is forever
tell everyone who you are
who you've met
where you went to school
nothing else is more important
repeat over and over
how high you've gotten
that's who you are, who you are
nothing else really matters
turn away from contradictions
ignore all lesser beings
spin ever tighter
your comforting cocoon
close off from extraneous emotions
the universality of human experience
is illusion
the quiet certainty of position
is reality.
* * *

I'm so smart, everyone agrees
tests have proven it
there's accomplishments galore
all the best people agree
that I am one of the best
so very far above you
and you and you and you
so sensitive and discerning
my refinement is beyond
your ability to conceive
you can barely even see me
I'm so smart so kiss my ass.
* * *

The curse of identity
dark side of meritocracy
illusion planted against the tide of life
trap for the unwary
dead end journey
spending life immersed
in unending shallow
conversations about hierarchy
shutting out glories of a world
far more intelligent
than any linear scale
a pernicious holding back
inner monologue round and round
repetition begetting certainty
sandcastle of dreams piled higher
defended to death with unscrupulous haste
frenetic everyday intricate waste
of a life derailed, joy postponed
frozen in contortion
on shimmering scales of imaginary worth
mystique passed down through generations
mirage so seductive so enticing
even when known to be hollow and false
enduring through all seasons
no matter lies and exceptions
no matter how many many are hurt
elevation from life is costly and hard
but it seems so obviously worth it to know
who and how much you are.
* * *

Hatred is denial
of the most essential
human birthright
indifference is unnatural
flotsam floating in the wake of hate
strenuous effort can achieve it
obscuring sight in eye and mind
of fantastic love and beauty
binding, driving human enterprise
its vital secret accessed only from the heart
imperfection is
the source and soul of intelligence
essence of perfection
but for illusions of escape
imagination has no limits
defining life as separation
completely misunderstanding
the world at large
inner self withers
seeming fragmented and absurd
wreckage spreads out far and wide
old friends lost, neighbors hostile
creeping stupidity infecting all
as they turn away
from life's shining light
denying equality's intricate balance
morals and freedom lose their roots
the drift is set for catastrophe.
* * *

If only bad folks did it
countering hate would be simple
eliminate source and scourge erased
over and over it has been tried
with ruthless thoroughness in righteous crusades
over and over the result's been the same
spreading contagion
splattering the landscape
deepening, embedding it
hardening hearts
generation to generation
although countering virulent acts
of the negatively obsessed
may necessitate employing
destructive means
a transition must be made
at some messy incomplete turning point
for the varieties of hate
are curable only
always only
by spreading love
the belief in love
practice of love
experience of love
imparting to the infected
ability to see
the most fundamental fact
of their existence
love is the default setting
and present reality
every moment of every life
blindness to this is
the heart of hatred
heart of darkness.
* * *

Hold onto light in disagreement
through struggle and strife remember
every person is
no matter what
essential to the puzzle of intelligence
bad ideas
pernicious intentions
may be maintained until the end
but even without change
their bearer is yet one of us
wrong ideas take part in good ones
neighbors you can never like
are members just as you
in the tribe of humankind
always look to see their spirit shining
accepting it as of your own
even if they do not.
* * *

To carry on in the face
of lies, deceit, defeat
is faith sensible
when evidence is bad
why go forward
when the whole world turns mad
knowledge of a wider truth
that carries on through time
and eventually, hopefully sometime
corrects itself, stands straight again
so abstract and austere
is often not enough
to stiffen spine and fix resolve
to keep on going against the wind
call it stubbornness or perseverance
a rising inner well of feeling
a strength that gathers beyond reason
to stand and be blown down again
such willingness may not make much sense
but sometimes only one way beckons
choices are long left behind
face to face with destiny
uniqueness has a price
mind incomplete, unsatisfied
standing against the wind.
* * *

Lost despite all reason
all thought trapped
in sticky quagmire
each step slowed by muck
fuzzy buzzing
obscures sight and sound
despair's sheer senselessness
defeats all logic
endless repetition
boring refrains
of hurt and humiliation
begin to fill both day and night
life slows down
an oddly comforting embrace
grows unnoticed
softly enfolding
uncertainty and doubt
in a stagnant sweet security
which must be lost to break free
back to living in the world
instead of the past
remaking connection
with the primordial life force
that rises within
participates and has presence
smelling, tasting, changing, loving
despite all reason.
* * *

Rise up
for an instant in a day
grow large
burst free
from the grip of darkness
holding your heart separate
in the shadow of death
let go
release yourself
into the floating
information continuum
joining you with the world
in all its rampant beauty
joining your heart
with mine.
* * *

8

And Magic in Your Eye

Largeness of spirit
springs forth spontaneously
with an opening of eyes
not summoned from within
not in spite of reality
neither sacrifice
nor some gift to the world
but an upwelling recognition
of some particular commonality
joining innermost aspects
of mind and being
with people, places, ideas
kitty cats and stars
acceptance to the core
of humanity's great gift
the smallness and particularity of self
opens the door
to the world outside
gardens teeming with variety
in which life takes place
allow yourself
to expand and grow
encompass flowers and neighbors
mountains and deserts
the good and the ugly
all of life begins again
in the instant
of embrace.
* * *

Humans do not choose to love
they fall
encounter
entirely new experience
on meeting someone else
a flower, vista, concept, song
or simply turning over a new leaf
as suddenly
hosts of tiny
sleeping tendrils
of feelings, ideas, pictures
they never knew
were in them
awaken
gather suddenly
in fresh coherence
intermixing aspects
of the world outside
in fresh embrace
rebirth rising
you and me
moment by moment
every morning
every day.
* * *

Those who find fortune and abilities
suited to their time and place
have a special kind
of solemn duty to respect
all whose capabilities seem less
who cannot throw as far, run as fast
sort berries quicker than the rest
helpless with machines
can't cook, tone deaf
can't do math, flummoxed by computers
the extra shy, not so funny
too short or tall, not serious enough
even those not good at self-promotion
notice them on the street
if you would see yourself
for crowds are never faceless
each acknowledgement
a recognition of the enormity
that is universal limitations
as their life so yours
the primal and personal
character of equality
provides entry
to worlds so large
you cannot see the horizon.
* * *

Something messed up
an arm or leg
false teeth, flat feet
glasses, bad heart
knees, hips, skin, hair
disabled
everyone's afflicted somehow
that new flaw
just one more in a list
of limits and anomalies
each implying
the partialness all share
thereby making uncomfortable
those embarrassed to embrace
inherent deficiencies
their own warm destiny
as bearers of diversity
the essential key
to human strength
everyone needed to
lend a hand
lend a mind
whatever they may have
coming together to form
the most powerful, successful
and intelligent entity
ever to arise.
* * *

When I am most awake
alert and clear
pollution free
depression abating
health flowing
when I feel the most me
a change occurs in what I see
though visual data remain the same
outlines, colors, movement, time
elevated senses play a part
sensing nuance in the day
enhanced awareness
of light and hue
can be a doorway
to seeing more
than meets the eye
beyond a shadow
wisp of hair
something jumps out
grabs attention
turns my head
meaning in a glance
shadows of memories
echoes of dreams
your face is shining
I can't look away.
* * *

When I feel
far from you
it ends up being
something in me
I've lost touch with
am less honest about
shrinking away from
the whole world
seems to fade away
but do not worry
it's just me
and when I recover
regain strength
and sense of self
new and old feelings
of connection with you
rise once more
just as they did
at first glance
and the next day and the next
when I'm most awake
awareness of youness overwhelms.
* * *

Nothing's ever over
ever really finally complete
fulfillment, closure, happiness
dreams unrealized and lost
all of life keeps moving on
loose ends haunt
all goals achieved
train arrived keeps steaming
hugs contain the morning after
with every breath
life mocks
attempts at freezing time
you're more than one thing
keep on moving
let happiness grow
our love evolve.
* * *

This old town
one page in its life
saw hundreds of faces coming and going
smiles and frowns, loves and dislikes
a world whose moments never repeat
now they're all gone, everyone I knew
all who were there, the entire collection
except that
by coincidence one day
from among so many
one appeared
we stepped aside
moved out of the mainstream
began a new world our own
while the old one
slowly fragmented away
those who comprised it
gone, died, moved on
that unique nexus
of life and love
lost in the flow of time
the set looks the same
but no one's there
all is empty
new faces no replacement
to those who remember
what went before
those shimmering heights of love and spirit
patterns giving meaning
left behind, half forgotten

leaving only
wandering traces
imprints in shadows
effecting maybe lives lived later
though they can have
no way of knowing
the beauty lost
infinities in each of us vanished
in the blink of an eye
revisiting the town I loved
from which you came
its reality, its life has disappeared
only the buildings remain.
* * *

How did I end up
in this strange form
rainbow face with uneven eyes
almost foreign feeling flesh
hanging on ungainly frame
what I really feel inside
is not the shape I inhabit
though it's changed by choices
and shapes experience in turn
it seems only to be as much me
as streets I walk down
and gardens of my delight
the whole collection of which
is the one life I have
consciousness spreading out
invading, creating the world I inhabit
of thoughts and dreams
connections reaching
through millions of minds
through the fabric of things
to the ends of the universe
and all of it is me living here
in my saggy baggy body
and ridiculous hair
a bit out of place, a disruption
a life.
* * *

Days occur when all is lost
friends seem strange
the center starts to spiral down
fragment and disintegrate
it's time to stop
turn around, think of you, look at you
let shimmering life appear afresh
let loving you reach deep inside
receptors hidden there engage
wake up inner self
renew connections to the world
my footsteps headed your way
trip on mysteries, new directions
ways of finding
what is real, what illusion
as I reach out
grasp ahold, take a ride
sometimes scary, sometimes slow
helping me to hold on tight
is life revealed
love's as certain
solid as the ground
and I feel it rise within me
every time I think of you.
* * *

Through all ups and downs
good times and hard times
when choices are bad
don't know which way to turn
keep an eye
on the basic template
present potential
always in the background
ready to leap
be seized upon and realized
look for new directions
through the lens
of information fields
where our lives find focus
only there is found
the contribution of humanity
our collective instrument
tool and weapon
hope and future
align with its improvement
increasing complexity
deriving strength
from inclusion and activity
of ever more minds not few
the beautiful equation
of love and intelligence
is the birthright of all
never forget
the default setting is love.
* * *

Did it happen if unseen
standards of evidence
can be considered
but in the end
you just have to believe
so much is going on
even though details
are hard to pin down
have faith that the world turns
tiny birds tweet in hidden forests
and myriads of people
are thinking, doing
living right now
a gigantic thunderstorm
gathering strength
intelligence accelerating
by nature out of sight
perceptible only
with the secret vision
sixth sense of love.
* * *

Palpable texture, utter reality
of our love together
stands proof that love exists
in spite of constant nattering
by neighbors and friends
trapped entranced
in persuasive cycles of denial
as all the while
love's sweet substance
flows smoothly
around and through them
from, among and out of them
our most precious, intimate
personal connections
joining everyone everywhere,
spreading out, expanding horizons
through trees and hills and puppy dog eyes
entwined in every nook and cranny
of your mind and mine
entirely mixed up
with language, music, impressions,
chance encounters, close relations
what we eat and how we play
all that and so much more
colors every glance we exchange,
longings coursing through our veins
and the utter enormity
clear blue reality of our love
shines in turn a light
outward through the universe
illuminating loves'
presence everywhere
surging current of life
defiantly challenging
all attempts to deny it.
* * *

Do your love her?
We've been married fifteen years…
inability to say the word
betrays ambivalence
nervousness is not surprising
there may be
wonderful companionship
family, common interests
naturally occurring commonalities
intricately exquisite complementarities
shared doubt, hesitation
searching and wanting
willingness to commit to life
all vital but not enough
human entanglements
have feelings at their core
so if and when it really is heartfelt
shout it to the hilltops
Yes I love her
I can't help myself.
* * *

I love the trees, the snow, the stars
little pitty-patter of kitty cat paws
and rolling down backstreets
strolling by shops
quick gestures of hello
glimpsing sly eyes
silhouettes of hope
a few pointless puzzles
ridiculous shows
some music strikes me
I don't know why
on and on
so many
personal peccadilloes
all adding to each other
and my love for you.
* * *

The place where life begins
things make sense
and building is good
the whole world's a garden
and one glance is enough
to fall in love with you
your wispy hair
and awkward bewitching gait
inspire the instant
when difference dissolves
space-time contorts
beyond all rules
closeness is infinite
the smell of your skin
defies illusion
obliterates cynicism
makes ridiculous every pretension
that life is not love
that you and I could ever exist
apart.
* * *

Information fields
flowers, grass, dirt and birds
infused with stuff
dreams are made of
in continuum with your mind
extension of it
independent of it
reach out and touch
feel air fall through fingers
infinity is right there
blink and you miss it
walk on, reach on
listening is joining
the enormity of reality
immediacy of magnificence
makes you part of it
essential and beautiful
let us live dancing
dancing through fields of life.
* * *

Eyes open
step forward
every moment
embraces the past
with shadows
stretching out ahead
laced with memories
childhood hillsides
warm blue waters
fears, dramas, dreams
faces long forgotten
each step mixing
bright colored shadows
with a million mind reflection
a whole world collection
a singing speaking kissing confection
from low spots and waysides
mountains, secret rooms
whispers of multitudes
echoing reverberating
joyfully resounding
drawing us inward and outward
filling our minds
with flowers unfolding
ever more textured, enticing
bright sunshine shadows
illuminate for me
the light in your eyes
shining warmer and closer
and more and more and more and more.
* * *

###